This book belongs to

_____

This book is dedicated to my children - Mikey, Kobe, and Jojo.
Mindset is everything.

Growth Mindset Ninja

A Children's Book About the Power of Yet

Ninja Life Hacks®
by Mary Nhin

If my mom asked how practice went, I would reply...

Before I grew my mighty brain, I gave up easily. I didn't understand that learning was the fun part!

I was easily discouraged from my failures...

Just as my friend had predicted, Ambitious Ninja won the difficult game!

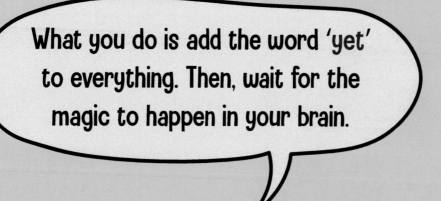

THE POWER OF
YET

I don't know how to do that... YET.

I can't do that... YET.

I'm not good at this... YET.

I thought about this for a while. I doubted adding just one little word would make a difference, but I decided I would try it, anyways.

The next day, my family was enjoying our weekly puzzle together.

I was having so much fun!

Then, I got puzzled over one piece. Out of habit, I shouted...

As soon as the words left my mouth, I remembered the magic of the word "yet," so I tried it...

All of a sudden, the clouds parted and my brain began to grow. It was making connections I couldn't see.

Before I knew it, I had figured out the puzzle all on my own!

Because of the Power of Yet, my brain continues to grow to this day!

Check out the Growth Mindset Ninja lesson plans that contain fun activities to support the social, emotional lesson in this story at ninjalifehacks.tv!

I love to hear from my readers.
Write to me at info@ninjalifehacks.tv or send me mail at

Mary Nhin
6608 N Western Avenue #1166
Oklahoma City, OK 73116

 @marynhin @officialninjalifehacks
#NinjaLifeHacks

 Ninja Life Hacks

 Mary Nhin   Ninja Life Hacks

 @officialninjalifehacks

Made in United States
Orlando, FL
30 September 2024

52133822R00020